MANLINESS

THE ROBERT MITCHUM WAY

JAMES SCOTT BELL

COMPENDIUM PRESS

Compendium Press
Woodland Hills, CA

INTRODUCTION

Real men don't appear out of seed pods. They begin
as boys who must be taught what it means to be
a man.

We used to teach them about manliness in
schools and at home.

Not so much anymore.

A hundred years ago, boys were encouraged to
read books that inculcated certain virtues, such as
love of adventure and bravery in battle. A suggested
reading curriculum for 8th and 9th grade boys
would have included *Captains Courageous* by
Rudyard Kipling, *Stories of Heroic Deeds* by James
Johonnot, and *The Spy* by James Fennimore Cooper.

It's difficult to find those analogues in today's
public school reading lists. This is actually a crisis,
as described in an article, "Why Boys Don't Read"

(July 1, 2015) by Linda Jacobson posted on the site GreatSchools.org: "Reading experts also point out that since the majority of teachers are women, they tend to assign books that are more compelling for girls; meanwhile, boys get negative messages from parents and teachers alike about the reading material they gravitate toward..."

Boys' natures need both taming and instruction. Without the former you cannot have the latter. If history teaches us anything it is that unbridled male nature is the greatest cause of evil and destruction.

Without a North Star of true manliness, the world suffers.

If you don't believe that, turn on the news.

If you still choose not to believe it, this book is not for you. Return it with my blessing.

But if you choose to understand what is self-evident, read on.

We are fast losing something essential in American life—the man who knows how to be a real man; who know how to treat women and children and community; who knows how to fight for what's right and honorable and who takes seriously his role as warrior and protector and father.

Please note, true manliness is not to be confused with Alpha-soaked testosterone. That is mere pose. It's not about chest-beating. It's not about strutting through a room to make sure everyone knows you're a man.

A real man doesn't need to pose.

He doesn't announce his manliness.

He lives it.

But first he has to know where to find it.

So where can a young man, or young father or mother, look for instruction in the true meaning of manliness?

I was lucky. I had a father from the Greatest Generation, a World War II Navy man, who was the son of a World War I Army soldier, who was the son of a preacher who was the son of a Civil War vet. That long line of men passed down the values and strengths that made America the greatest civilization ever realized.

But somewhere in the past sixty years that kind of tradition has been ridiculed by those who think there should be no such thing as manliness, that society would be better served by doing away with virtually any word that has "man" in it.

How's that working out?

In "The Sorry Lives and Confusing Times of Today's Young Men" [*Philadelphia* magazine, Feb. 20, 2012)], Sandy Hingston writes:

American men have gone astray because we've failed to provide them with a social construction of masculinity—an answer to the question "What makes a man a man?" That construction can be intellectual, as for Orthodox Jews, or more physical, as for Maasai warriors. But manhood can't just be something you age into. It has to be seen as an achievement, and aspired to. In the absence of such a construct, young men will provide their own—via street gangs or college frats or the eternal guyland of plasma TVs and fantasy football pools.

Before we as a society can offer that social construction, we have to decide: What exactly does make a man a man?

One day when I was cursing the darkness I happened to spot a candle.

It was a light known as Robert Mitchum.

Mitchum is one of my favorite actors, and this day there was a film of his on TCM I hadn't seen before, *The Hunters.* So I gave it a shot.

In the first scene (as described later in this book), Mitchum takes care of a man who's had too much to drink. It struck me that back in the 1950s that was something a man *just did.* Didn't need to think about it. It was a manly virtue. Simple as that. A little thing in this movie, but suddenly it spoke volumes.

And I wondered, where did men like this disappear to?

More important, how can we get them back?

The answer was suddenly obvious. One of the great resources we have for the training of boys in the virtues of manliness is the movies—especially the films made before 1970 or so, when attacks on manhood really took off.

And it occurred to me that Robert Mitchum was, in virtually all his films, representing some aspect of the quintessential American male. Even in films where he assumed the role of villain there is a lesson to be learned—the consequences of violating manly virtues. This is just as important for boys to appreciate as well. It's why the Greeks wrote tragedy. The ultimate aim was to warn men about the darker side of their natures.

I began to think about Mitchum movies and the lessons in manliness they taught.

And this book was born.

Who is it for?

First, for young men who are confused by the messages they're getting from society, college professors, and the myriad TV comedies that portray men —especially fathers—as little more than widgets from the doofus factory.

Second, for fathers who desire to teach and model for their sons the lasting virtues of manliness.

Third, for single mothers who, for one reason or

another, don't have the influence of a strong male figure in their sons' lives.

Finally, for women who complain there are "no good men out there" but aren't quite sure what to look for, even on dating sites.

What they're looking for is a real man.

You'll see what that looks like when you watch Mitchum movies.

ABOUT ROBERT MITCHUM

Robert Mitchum was born on August 6, 1917. He seems to have inherited from his mother a free-thinking, iconoclastic spirit. (I am indebted to Mitchum's biographer, Lee Server, for some of these insights. See his *Baby, I Don't Care* for the definitive treatment of Mitchum's life.)

He would always be his own man, which we might put down as the first rule of Mitchum manliness. You are responsible for yourself, and you should never bow the knee to any other man. You choose who gets your respect. In some situations you submit (e.g., the military). But always you think for yourself and remain true to the right ideals.

Mitchum described his boyhood as being one of "broken windows and bloody noses." There was hijinx and there were fights, and from this Mitchum learned not to back away when trouble started.

That training would come in handy when, at the age of fourteen, he left home and hopped on a freight train. He went on to live the life of a hobo during the Great Depression, which taught him how to survive on meager means and to get along with people--while beating up those who tried to take money or possessions away from him.

All this to say that when Mitchum finally turned to acting, he wasn't the product of some privileged background or soft-soap schools. It was natural, then, that he should start out as a gritty heavy in Westerns.

Mitchum was cast as an extra in a number of B Westerns starring William Boyd as Hopalong Cassidy. These were enormously popular and where Mitchum cut his teeth in front of a camera.

But then he got a break. He landed a role as a soldier in a 1943 MGM movie called *The Human Comedy*. In his short bit he flirts with some girls, one of whom is played by Donna Reed. His sexy charm and easygoing manner were on display for the first time, and it would mark his screen persona for the rest of his career--ruggedly handsome, a little dangerous, and never someone to mess with.

Mitchum the man, like all of us, was not perfect. but he had a central code that came through in every performance. He was an individualist. He refused to be manipulated into becoming another chunk of Hollywood beefcake.

For example, fresh from signing his first contract with RKO, the studio wanted him to change his name to the blander Robert Marshall. With absolutely no clout, Mitchum told the studio bosses where they could stick that idea. For that he was on the verge of being fired and blacklisted. Mitchum didn't care. Mitchum was his name, and he was going to keep it.

With some intervention by his agent, the studio relented.

Then he was told to get on the merry-go-round of publicity stunts, premieres, and staged photo shoots with starlets. Mitchum fought all this at every turn. An actor who was not gaining popularity would have been dumped. But by virtue of his performances in movies like *The Story of G.I. Joe* and *Till the End of Time*, Mitchum's rising star could not be denied. The studio tolerated Mitchum's behavior because they saw the dollar signs.

Mitchum with his good friend, Jane Russell

Mitchum was never awed by Hollywood glamour. Indeed, he often showed it contempt. Once, when he was loaned out to MGM for a movie called *Desire Me,* he was paired with one of the reigning queens of cinema, Greer Garson. On the set she was shown all the respect in the world, while Mitchum was treated like yesterday's newspaper.

In response, preparing for a kissing scene with Garson, Mitchum loaded up at lunch with onions and Roquefort cheese!

The one big hiccup in Mitchum's career––or perhaps we should say the one big toke––was his conviction for possession of marijuana. This was back in the late 1940s when reefer madness was associated with jazz musicians and crazed hipsters. Mitchum got caught smoking weed in a private home by two cops who were peeping through the window––no doubt tipped off by someone who wished Mitchum ill.

Even at the police station, Mitchum retained his detached bravado. When asked by the booking cop what his occupation was, Mitchum replied, "Former actor."

But with the help of the top Hollywood lawyer of the day, Jerry Giesler, Mitchum avoided a lengthy and embarrassing trial. The brilliant Giesler used a rare legal technique by submitting the case to a single judge for a ruling based on the grand jury transcript. While the judge found Mitchum guilty of conspiracy to possess weed, he gave the actor a scant sixty days in jail.

Still, that was a scandal. And if Mitchum had been under contract to anyone but Howard Hughes, he probably would have been Hollywood toast. But Hughes was a risk taker and didn't like anyone telling him what to do. He also had the keen insight to understand that a little bit of danger was now associated with Mitchum, and that would increase his box office appeal with the bobby-soxers. This was just before the age of Brando and Dean. Indeed Mitchum, one could argue, laid the groundwork for those two iconic bad boys. In any case, Mitchum's career soared to its greatest heights after his dustup with dope.

Yet even as he became one of the great stars of Hollywood, Mitchum never let that status go to his head. He treated everyone on the set, from grip to cameraman, with respect. The ex-hobo never forgot what it was like to be on the low end of the social hierarchy.

And while he was a better actor than many gave him credit for (because he made it look so easy), Mitchum never took himself all that seriously. Once, when asked what he looked for in a script, Mitchum replied, "Days off."

Mitchum married Dorothy Spence in 1940.

Theirs was one of the most durable marriages in Hollywood history, lasting 57 years until Robert's death in 1997. They had two sons, James and Christopher, and a daughter, Petrine.

Mitchum the man was perhaps best captured by the character actor Harry Carey, Jr., who acted with Mitchum early in their careers. "He was just an overwhelming personality," Carey said. "Big. Powerful looking. I don't know if they even had the word then, but Mitchum was *cool*. If they didn't have that expression he must have invented it, because he was just the coolest guy that ever lived. He had his own outlook on life and he didn't let anyone interfere with it."

ROBERT MITCHUM MANLINESS

Here they are. A selection of Robert Mitchum movies with lessons in true manliness.

If you can see the movies themselves, so much the better. You are in for hours of viewing pleasure.

But even without the clips, the lessons themselves are solid and can be easily understood.

Let's teach them again.

A real man refuses to play the patsy

In *His Kind of Woman* (1951, dir. John Farrow), Mitchum plays Dan Milner, a professional gambler down on his luck. Unbeknownst to him, a notorious racketeer who was deported has set in motion a plan to get back into the states by substituting himself for Milner, who bears a physical resemblance and has no close ties to anyone. The plan is to get Milner down to a Mexican resort, where a team awaits the racketeer (played with appropriate menace by Raymond Burr) to arrive by boat. The plan is to get Milner onto the boat so a plastic surgeon can drug him and use his face as the model for altering the racketeer's mug.

Get it?

I hope so, because this outrageous plot gets even wilder at the end.

Anyway, at the beginning, the gang sets Milner up so he'll have to accept a mysterious "job" for fifty grand. To do that, three thugs break into Milner's apartment in L.A. and wait for him. When he shows, they claim he has placed a bet on a horse with a local bookie and now needs to pay up.

Milner (because it's Mitchum) keeps his cool and says they've got the wrong guy and get out.

The lead thug puts out his hand for the money.

Now, being his own man, and being told by a thug what to do, Milner opts for an implied *No* by taking a lit cigarette and putting it out in the thug's palm.

This, of course, gets Milner beaten up.

And also incentivized to take this job in Mexico.

He knows he's being set up for something. This is called being a patsy.

A man does not stand still for being someone's patsy.

Milner begins sniffing around to find out what's happening. Along the way he has face time with a luscious singer named Lenore (Jane Russell), with whom he has instant chemistry.

Why? Because Lenore knows that Milner is his own man, unlike the rich Hollywood star Mark Cardigan (Vincent Price) who she is trying to land as a meal ticket. Cardigan is a big phony, playing heroes onscreen but needing constant ego feeding.

The plot takes some surprising turns, in no small part because Howard Hughes, the producer, wasn't satisfied with the original script. The result is something of a mess at the end, a change of tone from classic noir to the comedic, over-the-top performance of Price.

But the screen burns up whenever Mitchum and Russell (who became close friends) are on it.

At the very end it's clear that Lenore is his kind of woman.

But more to the point for our purposes, Milner is her kind of man—refusing to play the patsy and staying true to himself.

When a man on your team gets stinking drunk, you keep him out of trouble until he sobers up

A real man knows how to hold his liquor.

If he can't, he shouldn't drink.

There's nothing wrong with a social snort or two, so long as you don't get behind the wheel shortly after consumption—and so long as you don't bop someone in the snout in an argument over the New England Patriots and deflated footballs.

There was a time in America when a man handled certain major crises by getting drunk.

Rick does that in *Casablanca* when Ilsa, his long lost love, shows up at his café.

Many a movie has one man saying to another either, "What you need is a drink" or "I could sure use a drink."

America has had a long and sometimes troubling association with the John Barleycorn. It isn't going away, so a man has to know how to handle booze.

Robert Mitchum got drunk in several movies, most notably in *Heaven Knows, Mr. Allison.* There it is entirely excusable, as he is a Marine hiding out on an island with only a nun as a companion. So when he finds a bottle of sake he takes it all in. Even the nun forgives him for this. (More on this movie later.)

So a real man knows how to keep himself from becoming a souse who is a pain––or worse, a danger––to those around him.

But just as important, a man takes care of the men on his team who get falling down stinko.

In *The Hunters* (1958, dir. Dick Powell), Mitchum plays an Air Force major who has arrived at a base in Japan during the Korean War. His first night there he gets a drink at a local watering hole when another flyer, who has had more than a few belts, approaches and introduces himself. The flyer, Abbott, orders another drink and one for Mitchum.

Abbott invites Mitchum to join him for dinner with a beautiful woman. Mitchum accepts. In the cab ride to the restaurant, however, Abbott passes out. Mitchum goes into the restaurant to find the woman. She is, indeed, beautiful. That's because she is played by the Swedish actress May Britt, who was quite hubba-hubba. Mitchum explains the situation and escorts her to the cab. They get in, and she directs the cab driver to her place.

Once there, Mitchum puts Abbott over his shoulder and deposits him on the couch. May Britt offers Mitchum some coffee.

That's when she drops an important bit of info— she is Abbott's wife.

At which point Mitchum makes his exit.

Lesson: When a man on your team gets stinking drunk, it is your obligation to see to it that he avoids trouble, gets home, and sobers up.

In extreme cases, you will lay on some tough love

and try to recover the drunk's own manliness. (As John Wayne does with Dean Martin in the 1959 film, *Rio Bravo*.)

There are even times when a man should help a stranger.

In Raymond Chandler's best novel, *The Long Goodbye*, detective Philip Marlowe observes a man at a restaurant stumbling drunk and being unceremoniously left at the restaurant by the woman he is with. She drives off. Marlowe decides the man needs help, and takes him back to his place so the man can sleep it off. It begins a strange friendship that also leads into the twisting, turning plot.

Real men take care of their team members, even when they get out of control.

I was once at a high school basketball game when an opposing parent made inappropriate remarks at the cheerleader squad coach, a woman. This woman's husband, a bit of a hothead, ran over to the man and started threatening to shove basketballs up the man's rear canal. A physical clash was only seconds away. I stepped between them, holding the hothead back and keeping him from an assault charge. It also helped him save face, as he didn't have to back down on his own.

Perhaps I did this because I'd seen so many Robert Mitchum movies.

I can only hope so.

Know who your team members are and commit to watching out not only for your own interests, but theirs. Stick up for your guys when they need it. Get them out of harm's way if you see them walking into trouble. Don't get so ripped that you walk into the same trouble yourself.

Don't take another man's wife, even if she's in love with you

In the same movie, *The Hunters,* Mitchum falls for May Britt (completely understandable) and she falls for him (also understandable). There's a secret meeting, dinner, a lip lock. But both of them realize it's wrong. They must part.

But before they do, May Britt requests that Mitchum look out for her dipso husband, the one he helped get home from the bar. Mitchum promises to do so.

The lesson here, though is this: do not, under any circumstances, plant one on another man's wife. Not only does this violate the law of Mitchum, it runs afoul of a commandment of God.

A real man listens when both Robert Mitchum and God say the same thing.

A man keeps his word, even if he'd rather not

The husband in *The Hunters,* Abbott, makes a reckless move on a mission over China. He's part of Mitchum's team, but probably has a death wish (knowing that his wife is drawn to Mitchum). Against orders he goes after an enemy plane, gets shot up, and ejects by parachute into enemy-occupied territory.

Mitchum, the team leader, is supposed to return to base. The thing he's not supposed to do is land his fighter jet on the open ground and try to rescue the guy. But he made that promise to the guy's wife.

A man keeps his word, even though he'd prefer not to.

Mitchum lands and finds Abbott, as the enemy closes in.

Another flyer, a young hotshot played by Robert Wagner, also ejects so he can help Mitchum.

As the Air Force loses two prime jets.

But the promise! You keep it.

Mitchum and Wagner save Abbott, avoid the enemy, and eventually get help from some local peasants and get back to base.

Once there, Abbott pledges to his wife that he's through with the drinking and the self-pity. Mitchum has not only saved the guy's life, but restored his sense of true manliness.

In the last shot, May Britt is saying her final goodbye to Mitchum. As she walks back toward the hospital where her husband is, she pauses and turns for a final wave to Mitchum.

But he is not looking at her. He's looking up at the sky as a jet formation flies overhead.

For he is a warrior.

Which brings us to our next lesson.

A man listens to, and properly channels, his warrior heart

Mitchum manliness requires the proper channeling of the warrior heart.

When our natural fighting instinct is set in a good direction, such as destroying evil, it can save a civilization.

But when it is directed in a bad direction, like a bar fight over the Jets-Patriots game, it's juvenile and destructive.

Having a warrior's heart is not all glory and parades. It recognizes the hell of war, but does its duty anyway.

In Mitchum's star-making role in *The Story of G. I. Joe* (1945, dir. William Wellman), he plays Lt. Bill Walker, tough leader of C Company. It's based on the book by journalist Ernie Pyle, who is played by Burgess Meredith in the film.

Near the end, sharing a bottle with Pyle, Lt. Walker reflects on the life of the warrior, especially one in command. He remembers the names of the dead, the ones he has to write letters about. His face and voice are weary.

But it's the new kids, the ones with "fuzz on their faces," that haunt him most. He knows it's not his fault when they're killed, but "I feel like a murderer."

"Names and addresses. And the hills to be taken. They'd be simply amazed at the number of hills still to be taken ... If only we could create something good out of all this energy, all these men. They're the best, Ernie. The best."

"Yep," says Ernie. "It's a world the other world never knows."

Walker dies a warrior's death. It is sometimes the price of real manhood, because there is real evil in the world that will not settle for peace or diplomacy, but will only destroy if it is not stopped.

A real man respects women

The sad state of affairs (no pun intended) among men these days is an uptick in physical and sexual abuse. It's as if all the restraints put on men by religion and civilization over the millennia have been suddenly removed.

No, not even *as if.* It's happened.

Men are naturally sexual barbarians. They have to be restrained either by outside force—such as criminal laws—or inside character, which requires the strong nurture of family, community, or truly peaceful religion (and preferably all three).

Real men know how to respect women.

One of my favorite Mitchum movies is *Heaven Knows, Mr. Allison* (1957, dir. John Huston). It's the height of World War II, and Mitchum plays a marine corporal named Allison who has been adrift in a life raft and lands on a deserted island in the South Pacific. There's only one other occupant, a nun, Sister Angela (Deborah Kerr) who was there to help an old priest who died shortly after she arrived.

Now they have to survive together, catch fish, keep warm.

So here you have a full-blooded American marine alone with a beautiful woman who happens to be a nun.

She has not, however, taken her final vows.

Going through tough times with a beautiful woman, it does something to a man.

But Allison channels that desire in the proper, civilized way.

He tells Sister Angela when they get out of all this, he wants to marry her, take care of her.

He's not some smooth operator, just a guy who is putting his heart on the table.

Sister Angela is moved, but tells Allison she has already made a marriage commitment to Christ, and wears a silver ring as a token of it. When she takes her final vows, it will be a gold ring.

If this movie were made today, with two flavors-of-the-month, the guy would probably grab the nun and plant a hot one on her mouth, and the two would end up in a sleeping bag together.

But real men don't do that.

Allison accepts what she says and the two go on just as they had before, helping each other survive. Especially when a Japanese force lands on the island.

They make it off the island with mutual respect and honor.

There's another movie about respecting women, only done in a negative way. It's one of Mitchum's signature villain performances: *Cape Fear* (1962, dir. J. Lee Thompson). It's based on a great John D. MacDonald novel called *The Executioners*. The movie was remade by Martin Scorsese in 1991, starring Robert De Niro and Nick Nolte. (In a nice nod to the original, both Mitchum and Gregory Peck have small roles in the film.)

Mitchum plays a psychopath named Max Cady, who has just gotten out of a long stretch in the joint on a charge of rape. The chief witness against him was a lawyer named Sam Bowden (Peck), and Max has tracked this family man down in order to terrorize and eventually kill him.

It starts small, with harassment and stalking, but eventually Cady turns up the heat.

He kills the Bowden's dog.

He brazenly and publicly harasses Bowden.

He gets Bowden to lose his cool and, temporarily, his morals—Bowden hires thugs to beat Cady up. But Cady outsmarts them and Bowden is threatened with disbarment.

Eventually, Cady ends up on a houseboat with Mrs. Bowden (Polly Bergen). And we all know what he is going to do next.

But then, shocker, he manipulates things so he is alone with the Bowden's teenage daughter. And we all know what he is going to do next.

You need to watch the movie to find out what happens.

But this lesson needs to be hammered into men: your aggressive nature, unleashed, untamed, unmanaged, will result in the mistreatment of women, and you'd better get this straight right now, or your name might end up on a police blotter with sexual offender status slapped on you for life.

We'll see more things like the infamous Ray Rice video. Rice, a star NFL running back, was caught on tape in an elevator slugging his fiancé in the face, knocking her out cold. He then dragged her limp body out of the elevator and tried to figure out what he was going to do to get away with it.

He was cast out of football, out of his career, out of millions of dollars.

Because he did not live the manly virtues.

Real men respect women.

A man should make sure he doesn't fall for the wrong woman

Now we come to one of the signature Mitchum movies, *Out of the Past* (1947, dir. Jacques Tourneur). Considered by many critics to be the quintessential film noir, the film begins with a former PI named Jeff Bailey now living in a quaint mountain town. He's got a girl there, Ann, and they are destined for marriage.

Until the past shows up.

The past is represented by a thug, Joe, who works for a criminal, Whit Sterling (Kirk Douglas). Whit has been looking for Jeff, because he'd hired Jeff to go find a girl, the one Whit wanted to possess, but who ran out on him.

Jeff takes the job and goes south of the border to find her. He does.

And falls for her.

In film noir, it's never a good idea to fall for the femme fatale.

That's the lesson here, because it's going to cost Jeff Bailey the girl he should be with, the nice girl, the steady girl who will make a good wife and mother

Unlike Kathy, played by Jane Grier.

So Jeff tries to hide the fact that he's found Kathy. But then Whit and Joe show up at the hotel where the two of them are hiding out!

Jeff and Kathy manage to get back to the states and set up housekeeping for awhile. But then Jeff's partner spots them and he wants a cut of the money he thinks Jeff has. There's a fight.

Then Kathy shoots Jeff's partner dead.

Which totally stuns Jeff.

Yep, he fell for the wrong girl all right. A murderess, too.

Things do not end well for Jeff and Kathy. They can't. For it is a rule of film noir—and life—that if you get mixed up romantically with an immoral lover you're going to end up dead, or very, very sorry (like Dick Powell in *Pitfall*, where this straight-laced family man dallies with Lizabeth Scott, the legendary femme fatale, and almost loses his marriage to Jane Wyatt, but because he shows contrition he gets another shot at the end).

And if Robert Mitchum did not learn this lesson in *Out of the Past*, he certainly learned it in *Angel Face* (1953, dir. Otto Preminger) where he fell for Jean Simmons, with disastrous results. In fact, it leads to the next rule.

A man knows when the time's not right to flirt with a woman

Some men think they always have to be "on" around women. There are certainly appropriate circumstances in which to flirt. See, for example, Mitchum's bit as a soldier in *The Human Comedy* (1943, dir. Clarence Brown). He and two soldier buddies are out on the town when they're passed by a couple of pretty girls (one of whom is played by Donna Reed) The guys issue pleas for a meeting, and the two girls decide to allow it.

A man needs to hone his sense of when a girl invites flirtation.

The girls say they are going to the movies, and the men ask (not insist) if they might accompany them. Permission is given, and off they go to the cinema. The soldiers do not paw the girls during the movie. Real men do not paw women.

After the movie, the girls say it's time for them to go home. The soldiers do not argue, do not try to ply them with drinks. The girls allow them to give a tasteful kiss on the cheek. Real men do not insist on or try to force a tongue tango.

But a man who thinks he always has to put on his flirt face is really evidencing insecurity. Women much prefer a man who knows who he is and what he is about.

In *The Big Steal* (1949, dir. Don Siegel), Mitchum is teamed once again with his co-star from *Out of the Past*, Jane Greer. This time Mitchum plays an army payroll officer trying to recover the three hundred Gs a guy named Fiske stole from him.

Tracking Fiske to Mexico, he runs into Fiske's girlfriend (Greer) at the port of entry, then later in Fiske's hotel room––where she happens to be taking a shower.

Greer puts on a robe and confronts Mitchum. He tells her his name is Black, that he's an Army captain (this is a ruse). He then tells her to give up Fiske. Greer claims he's probably downstairs in the bar.

"You wouldn't be his wife, would you?" Mitchum asks.

"No, I wouldn't," Greer says.

With an approving up and down look, Mitchum says, "Mm-hm."

"I don't like that *Mm-hm*," says Greer. "I'm not his wife."

"If you were," Mitchum says, "I wouldn't be saying *Mm-hm*."

After a check of the room and belongings, Mitchum decides to move on.

Greer snaps, "Are you always so chivalrous to strange women, Captain Blake?"

Once more, Mitchum casts an appreciative eye at

Greer. Then he says, "We'll kick that around some other time," and leaves.

You see, there's a job to do: get the money.

Flirting will have to wait.

A man does not try to dally with two women at the same time

In *Angel Face,* Mitchum plays a former race-car driver and war vet now driving an ambulance in Beverly Hills. One night he and his partner get a call from a mansion in the hills where a rich woman has almost died from gas in her bedroom. She's okay, but as he's leaving Mitchum sees a beautiful young woman playing the piano in the living room. When he goes up to tell her everything's okay, she turns to him and looks exactly like Jean Simmons.

An angel face all right. Simmons was an absolute babe, and a tremendous actress, too.

Simmons is the stepdaughter of the woman upstairs, and, we'll later learn, hates her with a passion. In front of Mitchum she goes into hysterics, so Mitchum slaps her.

She slaps him right back.

This is how love begins in film noir.

(True story: The director, Otto Preminger, was notoriously hard on his actresses, and in this scene he kept directing Mitchum to slap Simmons harder, take after take. Finally, Mitchum had had enough, turned around and said, "Like this?" and slapped Preminger! The director stormed off the set and went to producer Howard Hughes and demanded that Mitchum be fired. Um, no. Hughes was not going to fire his biggest star. Preminger was forced to finish the film, and it has since become a cult classic, with some, like French critic Jean Luc-Godard, placing it among the best films of all time.)

As the ambulance drives away, Simmons hops in her sporty roadster and follows them back to the hospital. Mitchum tells his partner that he's going to see his girlfriend, Mary, who is preparing dinner for him. He goes across the street to a diner to call Mary, but she doesn't pick up the phone at first. As he's waiting at the counter, Simmons comes in, sits next to him and flirts a little bit. Mitchum, trying to be cool, flirts back.

There is no harm in a man being cool to a woman who flirts with him. But if he's got a date with his girlfriend, the rules change. It goes from cool to playing with fire.

The phone in the diner rings and it's Mary. Mitchum wonders why she didn't pick up the phone the first time. She says she was in the shower. As he's talking, Simmons sidles right up to him and puts her angel face near his.

This is where Mitchum makes his fatal mistake.

His girlfriend has dinner all laid out for them at her place. But Mitchum lies to her, says he's beat, that he's had a sandwich, and they'll see each other tomorrow.

Then he goes off in Simmons' roadster for an intimate dinner.

The girl asks Mitchum if he loves Mary. His answer is, "You ask a lot of questions."

Wrong answer.

They go out dancing.

Wrong move.

Simmons likes to dance, very close.

Simmons hatches a plan to sow doubt in Mary's mind and insert herself into Mitchum's life. She succeeds very well.

Mitchum lies to Mary once more, but she catches him in it right away.

Look, men, if you try to dally with two women at the same time, you're going to end up lying, and women always find out.

In this movie, Mitchum never quite makes up his mind. He is rather passive, going back and forth, letting his loins lead him.

A real man doesn't do that. He has rules and restraint.

In *Angel Face,* this eventually leads to murder, a trial, and one of the great shock endings in noir history. Treat yourself to the movie to find out what happens.

But only watch it with one woman.

A man knows how to play poker

The first time we see Sgt. Kelley (Mitchum) in Edward Dmytryk's *Crossfire* (1947), he's sitting in a hotel room with several of his Army buddies, playing poker.

Because men know how to play poker.

Even if he never gets into a big stakes game, a man should know:

- A straight beats three-of-a-kind.
- A flush beats a straight.
- A full house beats a flush.
- How to bluff.
- *When* to bluff.
- When to fold.
- When to leave the table.

When you are a young man, and go to college, the first thing you need to do is find a quiet place to study. The second thing is to get into a weekly poker game.

If you combine them both, you could call it Five Card Study.

When a man really messes up, he apologizes and makes things right

There's a manly film called *She Wore a Yellow Ribbon* (1949, dir. John Ford), starring manly man John Wayne. It's got manly lessons, but also one flaw. There's a line that Wayne, as Capt. Nathan Brittles, keeps repeating. "Don't apologize. It's a sign of weakness."

That's bogus. A real man apologizes when he messes up, when it's his fault. He stands up and takes his medicine. He doesn't make flimsy excuses.

And when he really messes up, he shows contrition by trying to make things right.

That, essentially, is the story of Paddy Carmody (Robert Mitchum) in *The Sundowners* (1960, dir. Fred Zinneman). Paddy is a sheep drover and shearer in the outback of Australia. He has a wife and son who share his nomadic existence. That's perfectly fine with him, for he is a wanderer by disposition. That makes his family "sundowners," folks who pitch a tent at the end of the day, and then pack up and move on.

Some men, you see, don't want to be tied down. These men are not usually good candidates for marriage, unless of course the wife is of the same mind. In Paddy's case, however, his wife Ida (Deborah Kerr) wants to settle with their son, set down roots on a farm. She's got her eyes on a nice property to buy.

Paddy is partial to an Australian gambling game called Two-up. It's played by betting on how two tossed pennies will end up when tossed. Paddy wins a race horse this way, a dream of his. With his son, Sean (Michael Anderson, Jr.) as the jockey, the horse, named Sundowner, wins a race. And money.

Ida is counting on this money to buy the farm. Paddy is not happy about this, but goes along. Until he loses all the money playing Two-up.

When a married man loses the family stake via gambling, that's called messing up. Big time.

Paddy shows his contrition by entering Sundowner in another race, to recoup the money. But the horse is disqualified, and the money is gone for good.

But Paddy resolves to make up for it all by dedicating his immediate future to saving all the money he can from his profession so the two can buy a farm after all.

When a man's in charge, he makes sure everybody knows where he's coming from

In *The Racket* (1951, dir. John Cromwell), Mitchum is police Capt. Tom McQuigg. He's put in charge of a district in an unnamed Midwestern city where the

Syndicate has taken over operations—though the local crime boss, Nick Scanlon (Robert Ryan) is none too pleased about it. Scanlon is old school, would much rather bump people off than buy them.

The one guy he can't buy is McQuigg.

The first time McQuigg addresses the officers in his precinct, he tells them he's got rules and they will be followed.

The first rule is that they are there to protect the taxpayers. That's their job. Never forget it.

And second, he will not stand for any dishonesty or "shenanigans." One violation of this rule and you're out.

A leader makes it clear to those under him what the standards are, and what the consequences will be for a violation of those standards.

Then McQuigg goes to pay a little face-to-face visit with Scanlon himself. He's going to make things clear to the thug, too.

Scanlon laughs in McQuigg's face. Scanlon can buy McQuigg ten times over. He has nothing but contempt for this "public servant."

When insulted by a bully, a man stays cool

McQuigg doesn't change expression. In fact, Robert Mitchum hardly ever changed expression. It's a good poker face rule of life. Never let your enemies know what you're thinking by the wrinkled brow or sweat on your forehead.

After Scanlon threatens McQuigg, the cop merely restates, "Stay out of my district."

Scanlon says he needs that district for the upcoming election, so McQuigg better get smart or "start to duck."

"Just stay out," McQuigg says, and leaves Scanlon standing there.

A man doesn't change his values in the face of a threat.

But a man isn't afraid to get hot when he needs to

When Scanlon kills a good, honest cop, McQuigg doesn't fly into a rage. He starts questioning the only eyewitness, a reporter. But the reporter is soft on a dame played by Lizabeth Scott (yep, here she is again!). She is streetwise and says if the reporter talks, the Syndicate will have him killed.

That's when McQuigg gets a little hot. He chews into Lizabeth Scott about the good cops who have been killed trying to protect people like her, and is that how she wants to live?

His speech makes an impression that will later lead to resolving the cop's murder, and getting Scanlon the punishment he deserves.

A man must teach his sons how to become men

There is no greater responsibility placed upon a man than to be a good father. He must love and cherish his daughters. He must help them flower and fulfill. He must understand them and respect them.

And his sons he must teach to be men.

Becoming a man is not automatic.

It requires the example and nurture of a father.

When that responsibility and bond is broken, families and society itself break down.

When the traditions of manhood are scorned and forgotten, it will not be long before an entire civilization devolves into chaos.

There is only one way to raise good men, and that is for fathers to take seriously their responsibility to teach their own sons. Daughters require a father to love and protect them. Sons require that, too, but also instruction in manliness.

When a father is not there to teach a son, the odds are greater that the boy will become either a criminal or a softie. He'll run with a gang that has a surrogate father figure, or he'll be taught feminine values only, and never learn the meaning, purpose, and necessity of manliness.

Wade Hunnicutt knew this. That's the character Mitchum plays in what may be his greatest perfor mance. The film is *Home from the Hill* (1960, dir.

Vincente Minnelli), about wealthy Texas patriarch Hunnicutt and his two sons, one of whom is illegitimate.

The illegitimate son is Rafe (George Peppard), and because of that birth Hunnicutt's wife Hannah (Eleanor Parker) has kept their natural son Theron (George Hamilton) to herself, part of a "deal" they made for her to stay in the marriage. But she has ever since denied Hunnicutt the marriage bed.

Well, Theron, now seventeen, is on the precipice of young adulthood and the discovery of girls. But he has not been schooled in any of the manly virtues. He's what the small town calls a "Mama's boy."

In desperation he turns to his father and begs him to teach him how to grow up.

Wade Hunnicutt takes over his tutelage, much to the outrage of Hannah.

In that culture there was a rite of passage called hunting. So Theron is taught how to handle a rifle.

A bit later it is reported that a wild boar on the loose, killing cattle. Some of the cattlemen turn to Wade for help.

Wade organizes a hunting party.

Theron begs to go along.

Wade allows it, and assigns Rafe to keep an eye on him.

Theron, deep in the woods, follows one of the

hunting dogs, and finds the dog in pitched battle with the boar.

Stepping up to the challenge, Theron shoots the pig and kills it.

The pride he feels is not something that can be had in any other way than by action. For a boy to become a man, he must learn this lesson. Filling a young man's head with self-esteem platitudes is not going to do the trick. Indeed, as Wade Hunnicutt understands, words of praise that are not earned are actually harmful to the formation of true manhood.

A man fights to keep his marriage together

My favorite scene in *Home from the Hill* comes at the big party Wade Hunnicutt throws to cook the wild boar Theron killed. Everyone's there in the big back yard, the pig is turning on a spit. It's a celebration for everyone but Hannah, who is still nursing her grudge.

Wade sees her on the porch. He goes to her for a private moment. He tells her how good she looks. He's clearly making an attempt to patch things up. It is the most vulnerable he has ever been in his life. And Mitchum shows his acting chops.

Hannah, however, gives him the cold shoulder.

It's devastating to Wade, who has endured this

for years. He makes some bad decisions because of it, from the bottle to the arms of another woman.

Both Wade and Hannah have grounds for divorce. But Wade does not divorce her, nor does she divorce Wade.

He keeps fighting for the marriage, and by the end of the film there is finally hope once again.

Too late. An outraged father who believes Wade impregnated his daughter (he didn't) shoots Wade dead.

Not every Mitchum movie is wrapped up in a nice little package.

Just like life.

Men need to get married. They don't need to be perpetual boys who impregnate girlfriends and walk away.

They need to get married, because that forces them to grow up.

We need more grownups. We've got enough boys as it is.

A man leads the assault

When duty calls, a man steps up. When there's fighting to be done, a man doesn't back down.

This doesn't just apply to war. It applies to family, friends, neighbors, and work.

In one of Mitchum's early films, *Gung Ho* (1943,

dir. Ray Enright), Mitchum has a supporting role as a WWII marine in a unit organized by Randolph Scott. Sort of like *The Dirty Dozen,* Scott puts together a special force for some tough fighting on Makin Island.

Scott interviews several marines. One of them is Pig-Iron Matthews (Mitchum). He has a history of getting into hot water for fighting. He explains to Scott that he grew up having to fight the other kids in the neighborhood. His instinct is to hit first and think later.

Scott explains that he's going to have to learn to do things the other way around. Mitchum accepts.

Later this unit is fighting a tough battle on a South Sea island. Mitchum has been put in charge of a group tasked with cleaning out a machine gun nest.

Mitchum tells his men that he's going to be the first one out. "I'll lead the assault. You cover me."

And out he goes, making up ground in a hail of machine gun fire.

Until he's hit.

In this kind of fighting, you know that chances are you're going to be hit.

It might even be fatal.

But it's your duty, and you do it.

You get a project at work, you do it.

If you're part of a team, and you're in charge, you lead the assault.

You gain the respect of your team.

And even if you go down, you still have a chance to recover.

The wounded Mitchum is brought back to camp. He's been hit in the throat, and can't talk. As he lies there he spots a Japanese soldier, thought to be dead, rising for one last shot at a couple of unsuspecting marines.

Mitchum tries to call out, but he has no voice.

The soldier readies his gun.

And from his stretcher Mitchum draws a knife and throws it into the soldier's back, saving his friends.

You never give up when you lead the assault.

In *The Longest Day* (1962, dir. Ken Annakin, Andrew Marton, Bernhard Wicki; prd. Darryl F. Zanuck) Mitchum plays the cigar-chomping Gen. Norman Cota, one of the leaders of the assault on Omaha Beach on D-Day. It was brutal going, with Allied troops trapped under heavy fire. At one point Col. Thomson (Eddie Albert) asks Cota if they should call in the ships to get as many survivors off the beach as possible.

Cota replies, "You think we brought these men here to watch some of 'em die and have the rest of them turn tail? Hell no we're not leaving. We're gonna get up that hill."

And they do.

A man protects the innocence of children

It is not manly to curse in front of children.

It is not manly to expose children to adult themes, which include sex and violence.

A man protects the innocence of children.

In *The Good Guys and the Bad Guys* (1969, dir. Burt Kennedy) Mitchum plays aging town sheriff Jim Flagg. It's around 1910 and the decency league of Progress has just expelled the ladies of the local cathouse, dispatching them by train.

A boy of about ten who lives at the same boarding house as Mitchum asks him why the ladies had to go. If they had done something bad, the boys says, Mitchum would have run them out himself.

Mitchum agrees.

Then if they were good, the boy wants to know, why did they have to go?

"Well, Billy, someday you're going to learn that people don't always agree on what's good and what's bad. These ladies were just practicing the world's oldest profession."

When the boy asks what that profession is, Mitchum clears his throat and says, "You see the

Lord made men and he made women, and he, um, didn't make them quite the same."

"Gee, I know that," says the boy.

The boy's mother interrupts and says that's enough questioning, and the boy complains that grown-ups "never tell kids nothin'."

Which is how it should be. You don't have to tell children everything. And you shouldn't. If they get too inquisitive about issues they're too young for, figure out a way to tell them nothin'.

A man rides shotgun

In *Young Billy Young* (1969, dir. Burt Kennedy), Mitchum plays Ben Kane, an old lawman who is out to find the murderer of his son. Along the way he meets up with an impetuous outlaw wannabe named Billy Young. He takes the hotheaded youth under his wing. As they ride together toward the town where the murderer might be, a stagecoach pulls up driven by a friend of Kane's. He's an old coot who is driving the rig alone. He's carrying some valuable cargo, which includes a woman, his only passenger.

Kane knows trouble is likely, so he has Billy tie the horses behind the stagecoach and get inside, and tells him to be ready to protect the lady should gunplay become necessary. Kane then hops up next to the driver, riding shotgun.

Sure enough, a gang of outlaws soon descends from the hills and chases the stagecoach. Kane and Billy manage to kill about half of them before the rest of the gang calls it off.

Men are expected to protect the vulnerable ones in their lives. When my son graduated from high school we took a family trip to New York City. I lived there years before. But it was all pretty new to my son. The streets were crowded, especially in Times Square at night. The four of us––my wife, daughter, son and I––were making our way down Broadway when one of those aggressive CD pushers made a beeline for my son. He touched his shoulder with his body. Instinct kicked in and I shoved myself in between. The pusher moved with us. Using my basketball skills, I stopped and boxed the guy out. My back was to him as my son and daughter and wife moved quickly along. I paused, then followed. That was the end of the push. If it hadn't been, I would have used another of my basketball skills, one involving an elbow.

The whole thing took about five seconds. I was riding shotgun for my family, and I always will.

Once a man takes on a tough job, he doesn't quit

In *Thirty Seconds Over Tokyo* (1944, dir. Mervyn LeRoy) Mitchum plays Lt. Bob Gray, a real-life Army Air Corps flyer who volunteered, along with about eighty others, for a secret mission. The only thing the volunteers knew was that the mission was going to be extremely dangerous.

It turns out that they were going to be the first squadron to bomb Japan in the early part of World War II.

In the movie, as the squadron heads for Japan on navy ships, Mitchum and the lead character, played by Van Johnson, have a conversation on deck. They reflect on what they are about to do, the moral question about collateral damage, but are not backing away from the danger. Johnson then wonders how many men will make it through. Mitchum says, "They figure about half."

Think about what these young men knew. Half of them weren't coming back.

But they did their duty. They were all in. Because once a man accepts a job, no matter how tough or dangerous, he sees it through.

Just to give you an idea of what the real Bob Gray went through, here's a bit from the website Doolittle-Raider.com. Note: Bob Gray was, at the time, just shy of his twenty-third birthday:

Crew of 3rd Aircraft - Plane # 40-2270 - "Whisky Pete" - Crew from 95th Squadron, 17th Group - (Bail Out)

Lieutenant Gray flew his B25 through antiaircraft fire to drop his bombs on industrial areas of Tokyo and strafe a military barracks before flying on to China. He ordered his crew to bail out when fuel ran out. During evacuation of the airplane Gunner Leland Faktor became the first casualty of the raid. Gray's navigator injured a leg upon landing and his copilot cut a hand while attempting to make a water bag out of his parachute's rubber cushion. The four survivors were assisted by local Chinese in reaching Chuhsien. The crew remained in the theater to conduct bombing missions. Robert Gray Field at Fort Hood, TX is named for the pilot of this B25 who was later killed in action.

Lt. Gray, who flew aircraft No. 3, could not make out the coastline in the rainy night. Not until he saw some lights through the cloud did he know that they had reached Chinese land and were exactly over the sky of a city.

As fuel was running out the bomber was flying over a mountainous area near Suicang County of Zhejiang province. Gray landed in a hillside and was shocked with cold sweat as he looked around and found that he was just a few steps away from a cliff. Gray and Sgt. A.E. Jones were found and escorted by local farmers to Quzhou.

Gray remained in China-Burma-India theater after Tokyo raid. He was killed in action on October 18, 1942 while on combat mission near Assam India.

A man takes a stand for freedom of the individual

In *Thunder Road* (1958, dir. Arthur Ripley) Mitchum plays Luke Doolan, a Korean War vet who earns his living running moonshine across the Tennessee border. A self-styled loner, Luke is a local celebrity in the eyes of the Harlan County mountain men who manufacture the liquor in hidden stills. With the aid of a souped-up sedan he evades the U.S. Treasury agents who yearn to nail the moonshiners for tax evasion.

The families who run the bootleg business begin to feel pressure from a racketeer named Kogan (Jacques Aubouchon), who aims to buy—or else destroy—all the stills in Harland County. The community initially decides to ignore Kogan's offer, but one by one they fold under pressure, sometimes violently. Meanwhile, Luke is approached by a Treasury agent (Gene Barry) who wants to use him to nab Kogan. Luke refuses to cooperate.

Despite Luke's loner status, his love for a nightclub singer almost persuades him to settle down. True to one woman only (another lesson in manliness), he rebuffs the advances of a local beauty who adores him, and promises to protect his brother, who idolizes him.

When a local transporter is killed in a car explosion intended for him, Luke realizes the seriousness of the situation, but refuses to stop deliveries. His younger brother, Robin (James Mitchum, Robert's son), is persuaded by a local working for Kogan to make a dangerous run, but Luke stops him before he completes his delivery, and vows to kill Kogan for interfering with his family. Before he can carry out the threat, Kogan is arrested for suspicion of murder and Luke breaks through a roadblock, fatally crashing into a power transformer.

Cool facts:

Some critics consider this the first—or at least the definitive—road/chase movie.

Luke transports whiskey in a hidden compartment adjacent to the gas tank. His car also has a button that releases an oil slick, causing the pursuing vehicle to swerve off the road, as in a James Bond film.

This was a personal project for Mitchum, who

came up with the original story, starred (with his son), co-produced, and co-wrote the awesome theme song. A year later, Mitchum recorded the ballad he wrote for the film. You can find it on YouTube.

A man knows when he must listen to tough talk

In *El Dorado* (1966, dir. Howard Hawks), Mitchum plays J. P Harrah, sheriff of the town. He is one of the fastest guns in the west. His old friend, Cole Thornton (John Wayne) is just as fast, and is a gun for hire.

After refusing to work for an unscrupulous cattle baron, Cole rides into town with a young charge named Mississippi (James Caan), only to find that Harrah has become a hopeless drunk and an object of ridicule in the town. He finds out that Harrah has fallen into this estate because of a woman (see *Don't fall for the wrong girl,* above). Cole finds out what happened. A woman came into town one day, with "big sad eyes and a long sad story." Just the kind Harrah is apt to fall for. Friends tried to tell Harrah the woman was no good, but he wouldn't listen.

Of course it turned out ... she was not good. She ran off with a whiskey drummer and Harrah turned to the whiskey bottle, and for two months he's been a sloppy, worthless souse.

Cole knows trouble is coming into town, in the

form of some gunmen working for the cattle baron. He also knows that Harrah is worthless in his present condition. With Mississippi's help, he pours a repulsive concoction down Harrah's throat that sobers him up in a particularly awful way.

When Harrah finally comes to his senses, Cole fills him in on what's happening in town. All Harrah wants is a drink. Cole looks at him with contempt, because that's what a man does to try to get another man's attention when the second man has hit the skids through the weakness of character. Especially in a Howard Hawks film.

It doesn't work. Harrah, dressed in his dirty, torn undershirt makes his way to the saloon and orders a bottle. As he stands there, the bad guys, seated around a table, laugh at him. There is nothing more humiliating for a man in a Hawks film than to be laughed at, and deservedly so. Harrah has reached rock bottom, and knows it.

He takes the bottle back to the sheriff's office, where Cole and Mississippi are waiting. He turns around with self-contempt in his eyes. "They laughed at me," he says.

Cole says, "They've been laughing at you for a couple of months. You just haven't been sober enough to hear it."

Tough talk, John Wayne style. Which is what a man who has lost his dignity needs.

But he has to choose to listen.

Harrah has reached the crossroads. He can take the bottle to bed with him or ... he throws the bottle to the floor. He grabs his gunbelt. "I'll show them!"

Good. He's recovered his fighting spirit and sense of self.

But Cole knows Harrah is a shell of his former self. Until he fully recovers, he's likely to get shot.

Still, Cole comes alongside—even though Harrah tells him not to. He's keeping an eye on Harrah, but also letting him make the decisions as sheriff. (It's a rare thing for a man to have a friend like this, who knows his deepest need, and finds a way to provide it without making it seem like charity work.)

Shots are heard at the saloon. An innocent party has been wounded, and three men have run off into the night. The old Indian fighter, Bull (played by the great character actor Arthur Hunnicutt) knows it's a trap. The three men are lying in wait for the father of the victim to come after them.

But Harrah steps in as sheriff, and forbids it. He's taking responsibility again. He sets off to arrest the men. He doesn't ask for any help, but Cole and Mississippi and Bull go with him anyway.

Guns blaze.

The good guys win.

J. P. Harrah is restored to his former self, town

sheriff, newly respected. Because when confronted with his sorry state by a good friend, he dug down deep and chose to mount a comeback, man style.

A man knows how to handle a brush off

You're not always going to be a hit with a lady. In fact, sometimes you're going to get the brush off.

In which case you can react in one of three ways.

a) like a whimpering poodle;

b) like a snarling pit bull, or

c) like Robert Mitchum.

Correct answer is c.

In *Macao* (1952, dir. Josef von Sternberg), Mitchum plays an American ex-pat on his way to the Chinese peninsula. In the first scene, a sweaty man is trying to make time with the luscious Jane Russell on a boat headed to Macao. It turns out that Russell wangled a ticket out of him in return for the promise of "a few laughs."

The sweaty guy is ready to collect, but Russell resists. When he gets physical Russell throws a shoe at him. The shoe goes sailing through an open window and hits Robert Mitchum in the head.

That brings Mitchum into the room asking which one of them is Cinderella. The sweaty guy tells him to get lost, and when Mitchum tells him to cool off the guy takes a swing at Bob, who lays him out with one punch.

Now Bob is with the luscious Jane Russell himself. After a little banter he does one of his patented moves, and plants a big kiss on her.

She says, "Now we're even," and walks out on him.

Mitchum watches her go. He doesn't whine, he doesn't run after her and drag her back in the room.

He simply raises his eyebrows and moves on.

That's how you handle a brush off. Not with sweat or desperation, but with a shrug.

A man who chooses to drink knows that one martini is enough

If a man chooses to drink socially, he needs to know his limit. Drunkenness never becomes a man. Or a woman, for that matter.

When it comes to the martini, a man takes to heart the proverb of the American writer James Thurber: "One martini is all right. Two are too many, and three are not enough."

In the epic television mini-series, *The Winds of War* (1983, dir. Dan Curtis, based on the novel by Herman Wouk), Mitchum plays Victor "Pug" Henry, a naval attaché in the years leading up to World War II. In this role, in which he is unofficial eyes and ears for President Franklin Delano Roosevelt (Ralph Bellamy), Henry meets with the key world leaders—Hitler, Mussolini, Churchill.

In the episode titled "Defiance," Pug Henry is summoned to the White House for a meeting with President Roosevelt. Henry is there to get instructions on what the president would like him to observe next.

Roosevelt wheels himself (for you youngsters who never got a good history education, Roosevelt suffered from polio and was in a wheelchair a good part of his adult life) over to a table and mixes martinis. He shakes them and pours, then drops an olive into each of three glasses, for Eleanor Roosevelt has come in to join the men for cocktails.

Henry sips his drink and says, "This is an excellent martini, Mr. President. It sort of tastes like it's not there at all, just a cold cloud."

Roosevelt answers, "You have just described the perfect martini."

So let's make clear what goes into this classic cocktail.

First and foremost, gin. You cannot make a martini with vodka. Instead, you should have to ask for a "vodka martini," but civilization has diminished to such a point that it's almost assumed now that a martini was vodka-based first. A vicious canard.

To the gin is added just the right amount of dry vermouth. No more than 1 part vermouth to 6 parts gin. In the 1920s and '30s, when Roosevelt was doing most of his imbibing, the ratio was more like 1:3 or 1:4. Winston Churchill, the great contemporary of Roosevelt, anticipated the decline of vermouth when he said that a martini should be made with ice-cold gin and a bow toward France. Alfred Hitchcock, the great film director, said that one should pour in the gin and then look at a bottle of vermouth across the room. (This quote is erroneously attributed to Churchill, but the two men obviously agreed.)

You can pour these ingredients into a glass pitcher or silver shaker. To the pitcher you add ice and stir (James Bond would walk out on you, though). The preferred method is to put it in a shaker and then make that satisfying sound you hear in the finest restaurant bars.

I will allow that some purists think shaking the gin can "bruise" it. Um, no. But if that is your flight of fancy, stir away.

Your martini glasses should be chilled, in the freezer, for at least fifteen minutes. Thirty minutes or more is better.

Shake and pour, then add one, and only one, olive. Two or more olives disturbs the equilibrium. However, there are those who really, really love olives, so if you want to let that overpower the "cold cloud," there's nothing to stop you. You can even order it "dirty" with some extra brine, but that is very close to what the barbarians drank just outside the gates of Rome.

Now, there is flexibility concerning the dryness of a martini.

A dry martini has less vermouth, and a very dry martini almost none at all. For the latter, one should pour a thimbleful of vermouth into the glass, whirl it around, then pour it out.

By the way, some purists argue that martini should be capitalized, as it is short for Martini & Rossi vermouth. The choice is yours.

As is how many you have.

President Franklin Delano Roosevelt, First Lady Eleanor Roosevelt, and Commander Victor "Pug" Henry all have just one martini.

"If a man doesn't know what he's doing, or where he's going, the best thing for him to do is just back up and start over again."

So says widower Matthew Calder (Mitchum) to his young son, Mark (Tommy Rettig) in *The River of No Return* (1954, dir. Otto Preminger). Calder had served a long stretch in prison for killing a man by shooting him in the back (we later find out it was to save the life of his friend) and has now gathered his son to come live with him on his modest farm by a big river and lovely mountain ranges.

In his way, Calder is telling Mark that there may come a time when a man realizes he's not going anywhere and has to take stock. If he's off in a wrong direction, it's time to back up and start over, "from the ground up," and do something useful. Like make your own living by producing good things.

Not that it's always going to be easy.

Down the river one day comes a raft. On the raft are a gambler, Weston (Rory Calhoun) and a saloon singer, Kay (Marilyn Monroe). This gambler is trying to get to Capital City to register a gold mine. When Calder won't lend him his horse or his rifle (the one thing that can stave off the hostiles in the hills around him), Weston knocks him out with the rifle butt and "borrows" the horse.

Kay, incensed, stays to help Calder recover.

But the Indians have been watching. They start down toward Calder's place. The only escape is that raft. As the hostiles set fire to Calder's house, he and the boy and Kay barely escape down the River of No Return.

20th Century Fox, the studio behind this expensive, A-list picture, knew what the audience wanted. The scenery—by which I mean, Marilyn Monroe. Nothing like Marilyn Monroe in tight jeans and a camisole getting wet on the raging river. And in CinemaScope yet. Talk about mountain ranges!

Side note: According to Mitchum's biographer, Lee Server, Mitchum did not see Marilyn the way so many Hollywood types, and at least one president, did—as a piece of flesh to be bedded at the earliest opportunity. He saw her the way she was, a vulnerable and somewhat disturbed young woman who was having trouble dealing with sexpot superstardom. He treated her kindly, like a big brother, even though she could be troublesome on the set. (It didn't help that the director, Otto Preminger, was a notorious martinet.)

And when she needed a kick in the acting pants, Mitchum gave it to her. Marilyn insisted on having her drama coach, a woman of dubious background, on the set. It didn't help that this woman was giving Marilyn terrible acting advice about enunciation. That's why Marilyn looked so odd sometimes, moving her lips in exaggerated ways as she tried to make each word perfectly clear in that whispery voice.

Mitchum got fed up in one scene and yelled at her to just start acting "like a human being." That was Mitchum's style, and he at least got Marilyn to tone down the lip thing.

The movie ends when Calder, Mark, and Kay catch up with Weston. While Mark is inside a general store checking out the rifles, Calder goes out to meet the gambler. Who pulls a gun on Calder and fires.

Calder dives behind some bags, but it's no good. He's weaponless. Weston step up and takes dead aim.

And is shot through the back.

Mark, in the store, did it to save his father's life. Now he understands what his own father did years ago.

Marilyn gets to sing one more saloon song, then Calder carries her off to his buckboard to take her back to the farm to live with him and Mark.

A real man takes care of his family

A real man steps up and does what he has to do to take care of his family—wife, children, those dependent on him.

A real man does not impregnate women then go off to impregnate more women. Those kind of "men" are cowards, juveniles, not worth the dirt under the fingernails of real fathers.

Take Eddie "Eddie Fingers" Coyle. That's the Mitchum character in one of his best performances, *The Friends of Eddie Coyle* (1973, dir. Peter Yates). Eddie is a working stiff truck driver who also moonlights as a gun middleman for local criminals. He's got a wife he loves, and who loves him, and three kids. It seems like a stable, albeit lower middle-class existence, until Eddie's past catches up with him. As the story opens, Eddie is facing a two-year prison stretch unless he can make some sort of deal with the prosecutor.

The one thing Eddie can't stand is the thought of his wife and family going on welfare. (Imagine that! There was a time when men believed it wasn't honorable to be dependent on the government teat.) So he agrees to be a one-time stoolie.

That's not a good thing to be, of course. But it shows the moral ambiguities real men sometimes have to face. When those happen a man has to have a North Star to steer by, and Eddie's is his dedication to his family.

Well, things don't exactly go as planned. After Eddie delivers his goods, the fed he's dealing with tells him he's going to have to keep on being a stoolie. No one-time deal here.

Thanks, fed. Way to go back on your word.

The story of Eddie Coyle does not end up all sunshine and roses. It's a hard world he inhabits.

But real men understand life *is* hard, in various ways. And what they do is this: they protect, defend, uplift, teach, and love their families.

A man knows how to be charming

It used to be that a man worked on his charm. That was an ideal. I mean, Sleeping Beauty did not fall for Prince Doofus, right? The nurturing of grace and wit and ease of motion was something men used to strive for.

Today, I see a lot of posing. Guys with default macho walking into bars with unsmiling, hard-ass looks on their faces, as if this is what it means to be cool.

I laugh at them.

Robert Mitchum would have found them boring.

Because Mitchum had charm in an otherwise forgettable little film called *Girl Rush* (1944, dir. Gordon Douglas). This was a B comedy-Western made by RKO, right before Mitchum hit it big with his supporting turn in *The Story of G. I. Joe.*

In this film, Mitchum plays a cowboy named Jim who gets involved with a couple of stage show impresarios played by Wally Brown and Alan Carney. They run a stage show with a full cast of dancing girls, who are threatening to quit because they don't get paid enough.

So the two producers hatch a scheme to get a group of investors, including Jim, to pony up dough to take the girls to the girl-less town of Red Creek. Only thing is, they've told the girls they're on their way to New York, and the big time!

Well, the plan goes awry out on the trail when

Jim finds out that the women have no idea they are to stay in Red Creek. The girls figure out they've been lied to, and the men start looking for Brown and Carney to string them up.

It looks like it's going to be one big disaster for all concerned. Then Jim takes the lead girl, played by Frances Langford, aside in the moonlight and works his charms. He works them so well he comes in for a kiss, which she happily accepts.

By the way, a real man does not ask for permission to kiss a woman. That is only in the doofus rules. A man goes in for a kiss, and if the woman refuses or pulls away, he accepts it with grace. But he does not give her an informed consent form beforehand. (Unless, of course, he is a young man going to college, in which case all the rules have been rewritten by chuckleheads.)

This charming kiss solves everything. Frances Langford agrees to go to Red Creek with her girls and do a show. In the next scene, Mitchum and Langford are sitting on a covered wagon together as they roll towards the town. Here comes some more charm:

Mitchum says, "We'll probably make it in another hour or so."

Langford says, "I'm in no hurry. I'm enjoying the ride."

To which Mitchum says, "I wish I'd picked a longer trail."

Just the right line, just the right delivery. That's not an easy skill to pick up. It takes practice. There will be some flubs.

But the charming man knows how to say something charming and not over play it, and if he falls flat, he just moves on.

A man can pour on the charm in any situation. When Jim is alerted that thugs are waiting in Red Creek to shoot the men and take the ladies, Jim hatches a plan to dress them all in drag. So on they come into town and the men of Red Creek think it's only the women. They invite them into the saloon. And every one of them is hit on. Since Mitchum is tall and broad in the chest—in a manly sort of way, of course, a tall cowboy comes over and says, "You're for me, ma'am, I like 'em big."

Ever the charmer, even in drag, Mitchum replies, "Well, they don't come too big for me either, bud."

Works like a charm. The cowboy takes Mitchum over to the bar to buy him (her) a drink!

A real man sometimes has to kill bad guys

One of the great dangers (not just tragedies, but dangers) of modern culture is the crazy idea that "violence is never the answer." In a story in the *New*

York Times business section, October 27, 2015, "Sweeping Away Gender-Specific Toys and Labels," this self-destructive notion is given the lie by human biology. The idea is that there shouldn't be "boy specific" or "girl specific" toys. The problem with that is that there are still boys and girls, despite what college wants to teach the kids.

Mattel did some massive research about this, regarding action figures, and guess what? "For boys," the research showed, "it's very much about telling a story of the good guy killing the villain. There's a winner and a loser. Girls wanted the action and the battle, but would tell us: 'Why does the good girl have to kill the villain? Can't they be friends in the end?'"

What we need to do is take these girls on our knee and say, "No, sweetheart. Sometimes villains have to be killed, or they will kill you and your mommy and your daddy. You see, villains don't want to be friends. They want to kill good guys."

And if the girl does not like that, and doesn't want to play that way, then let the boys at it.

Because boys are wired to kill bad guys. They just have to be taught when, and how.

Usually it's when they become policemen, or soldiers.

But society will cease to exist if we think villains

should never be killed, but only turned into our friends.

You should ask Neville Chamberlain about his plan to make friends with Hitler.

This naïve, childlike wish is what fairy tales and adventure stories have traditionally been about. As G. K. Chesterton once remarked, "Fairy tales do not tell children the dragons exist. Children already know that dragons exist. Fairy tales tell children the dragons can be killed."

Robert Mitchum knew you have to sometimes kill the villains, especially in a movie called *Man with the Gun* (1955, dir. Richard Wilson). Mitchum is a guy named Tollinger who gets hired to bring some law and order to a town. Because he can handle a gun and therefore bad guys with guns.

The bad guys don't like that. So they get together and try to kill Tollinger.

He kills them instead.

This is a familiar formula for Westerns of the 1950s.

Now, the thing is, Tollinger doesn't *want* to kill. He would rather make friends! Or at least, get people not to wear their guns in town.

But guess what? Some bad guys don't want to do that. They don't want to obey the law. They'd rather commit crimes and make people miserable and sometimes commit murder.

Making nice with them doesn't work.

Ever.

Which is why you need a Tollinger. Or a policeman. Or a soldier.

Because if you don't have those, soon enough you'll be dead yourself, and your society will be, too.

A man knows war is hell, and hell doesn't make friends

And sometimes the killing of bad guys happens in war.

In *One Minute to Zero* (1952, Dir. Tay Garnett), Mitchum plays Colonel Steve Janowski, stationed in South Korea at the start of the Korean conflict. He's training South Koreans in the use of the bazooka against enemy tanks. But he's also in charge of getting civilians the heck out of there, because trouble is imminent.

One of those civvies is a fetching United Nations worker played by Ann Blyth. She argues with Mitchum about the hostilities. She's from the U.N. you see, and the U.N. is full of nice feelings and intentions. When she's told that the communist armies are already mobilizing, she gives this priceless response: "You can't honestly believe they're planning war."

Mitchum says, "The plans are made in Moscow."

"They wouldn't dare," she says. "They'd be taking on the whole world."

"That stopped Hitler?"

To which she gives another priceless rejoinder. "This time it's different. This time we have the United Nations!"

"Hope does not win wars," Mitchum says, then turns around to go back to real work, training the soldiers.

A bit later, Ann refuses to get on the last plane out of there, so Mitchum picks her up and slings her over his shoulder, and puts her on the plane himself. The plane crew shuts her in.

Mitchum's sergeant, played by the great tough guy actor Charles McGraw, says, "I once got in serious trouble throwing a dame around like that."

"Oh?" says Mitchum "What happened?"

"She almost married me."

A mere second later, a North Korean bomber blows up the very building where Ann was standing minutes before.

Thus, the man who knows that hell does not want to make friends saves the life of a naïve U.N. worker (which may be redundant).

Around this time in the real Korean conflict, Soviet-backed guerrillas were mixing in with refugees fleeing the North. So among the refugee population made up of old men and women and children were bad guys smuggling in guns, knives, and other weapons—not to mention themselves—into the South, with one intention: to kill as many American soldiers and South Korean nationals as possible.

The movie revolves around that infiltration, and puts the inescapable moral quandary directly in the hands of Col. Janowski. Here is the question: if you know that refugees are being forced to march by the Communist guerrillas threatening their lives and families, and you know that machine guns and ammunition are being brought in by carts and even baby carriages, what are your choices?

Janowski orders leaflets and loudspeaker announcements, telling the refugees they must stop. But the guerrillas keep forcing them to move.

Reluctantly, Janowski orders mortar fire over the heads of the refugees.

Still no stopping.

The last and most troubling decision must be made—fire on the refugees themselves.

Horrific. And recognized as such. And you may say, like Ann Blyth does in the film, that it cannot be justified under any circumstances.

Only when Blyth sees what the commies have done to some of the American soldiers does she get the picture.

When hell is your enemy, there are not perfect

answers. But men have to make a decision. The people in the stands, don't.

Sometimes those decisions are indefensible, such as what happened at My Lai during the Vietnam War.

Other decisions are mired in a gray, moral area which fighting hell seems to demand. Such as the decision to drop the atomic bomb on Hiroshima and Nagasaki to bring an end to World War II.

You can't make nice with hell. You can't close your eyes and wish it away, or hope that hell will decide to play rainbows and unicorns with you.

Hell wants to kill you.

A man knows this.

After giving ample warning verbally and by dropped leaflets to the communist-infested refugee lines, Mitchum orders warning shots to be fired.

When the Communists, who are forcing the refugees to march with guns in their backs, refuse to turn around, the fateful order is given. Artillery hits the line killing both communist and innocent alike.

As fate, and the screenwriters would have it, Ann has just driven up to see Steve, and witnesses the carnage. She is appalled. Steve, going through his own moral quandary, orders the sergeant to get her the hell out of there.

It is not until later, when she is shown what

commies do to prisoners, that she realizes the enormity of Mitchum's decision.

A man doesn't let age stop him from doing what he wants to do

Mitchum kept on acting, almost to the very end (he died at age 79 in 1997). In his later movies he proved the above dictum. He did not let age stop him from doing what he did—act.

Not all of the movies, however, were, shall we say, classics.

Some were complete Cheez Whiz.

Like the 1995 film *Woman of Desire* (dir. Robert Ginty). This was a vehicle for the actress Bo Derek —*all* of Bo Derek—who plays a seductress who accuses one of her lovers of rape and murder.

This guy, played by Jeff Fahey, needs a lawyer.

Cue Robert Mitchum as an old criminal attorney about to retire. He takes the case.

Methodically he goes about investigating, but having doubts about his client's story.

Mitchum knows the guy is gaga for Bo, but also that Bo is a lying seductress.

So when he has the chance to question Bo under oath, his precision and insight into human nature gets to the cool, calculating vixen, who shows her stress by breaking the glass of water she's holding.

Her hand starts bleeding and she has to be ushered out of the courtroom.

By this time Mitchum—whose weathered features at this point in his career make him a dead ringer for a basset hound—sniffs out what's really going on. The client insists that Bo loves him, and Mitchum tells him, "Funny, isn't it? You pretend to believe something long enough and it finally becomes true for you."

(Remember, don't fall for the wrong girl!)

And don't lie to yourself. Face the truth, whatever it is.

Again, don't let age stop you from doing what you do. Sure, physical limitations will creep up, but you fight them as much as you can. You do not go gentle into that good night.

The American author Herman Wouk has written some of the most popular novels of all time, including *The Caine Mutiny* and *The Winds of War* (the TV series which starred Robert Mitchum). At the age of 97, Wouk signed a contract with a big publisher for yet another novel, *The Lawgiver*. And to top that, the same publisher has come out with *Sailor and Fiddler: Reflections of a 100-Year-Old Author*.

Keep doing what you do, man.

A man does not show up buzzed at a new gig

A football player named Johnny Manziel made headlines when he was drafted into the NFL, and not for his play. It was for his arrogance, his flashing of the money sign to brag about how rich he was—all before he'd played a single down. (Here's a bonus note: a real man does not brag about how great he is before he proves it, and not even if he does. Braggadocio is not just classless, it reveals an inner insecurity.)

Well, Manziel also had a drinking problem and a lousy rookie year for the Cleveland Browns. While no one claims he ever played while buzzed, being an NFL quarterback, especially a rook, means you prep 24/7 during the season.

Manziel blew it because of booze.

So he went to rehab in the off season, returned for his second year. He was told by the coaching staff to stay clean and sober.

Then a video hits the internet, showing Manziel at a club during a bye week, with a bottle of champagne in his hand.

Manziel made things worse when he tried to convince the coaches that it was an "old" video, and getting his friends to back up the lie.

There you have it. Letting booze wag your tail not only ruins your gig, it makes a fool out of you.

Sometimes, it's even dangerous.

In *What a Way to Go* (1964, dir. J. Lee Thompson),

Mitchum plays against type as an urbane business titan complete with private jet. The conceit of the film is that Shirley MacLaine marries men who are poor but love her, then they get rich and die. So when she marries Mitchum, she is afraid all his money will lead to disaster.

She convinces him to cash in and buy a farm, returning to his childhood roots. Which includes getting a cow named for one he had as a kid, Melissa. He also gets a bull named Melrose.

The locals welcome this couple which means, among the men, a jug is passed around. Mitchum nips a bit too much then goes to the barn to milk Melissa.

He sits on a stool and reaches underneath and yanks.

And then realize he has just attempted to milk Melrose.

He shouts, "Forgive me!" just before Melrose kicks him through the barn door and through the air to his untimely death.

If you get a new gig, or a new responsibility, you don't show up buzzed. You won't just blow things, you might end up getting kicked through a wall.

A real man has muscles

A man should be strong physically. This doesn't always mean bulky. But it does mean strengthening those arms.

There was a time when the male ideal included having a certain kind of physique. Robert Mitchum had it. The V shape with broad shoulders and big chest, and muscular arms for heavy lifting.

Somehow another shape has gained acceptance in our culture. A sort of creamy smoothness combined with a spindly softness.

Metro, not manly.

Hipster, not Homeric.

A man needs muscles.

In *Ryan's Daughter* (1970, dir. David Lean), Mitchum plays Charles Shaughnessy, a quiet schoolteacher in a small Irish village. He just happens to be handsome and have muscles. So a young girl from the town, Rosy Ryan (Sarah Miles), forms this fantasy about him. She's all hopped up on romance fiction and decides the much older teacher is her ideal. She throws herself at him and he finally agrees to marry her.

Rosy's unrealistic expectations eventually lead her to an affair with a wounded British officer, and the consequences thereof.

But in one scene this idealistic bride watches as Charles, shirtless, chops wood. That's what a real man does, by the way: chops wood when he has to. And he can't do that without muscles.

Rosy pants after Charles when she sees those muscles in action.

All other things being equal, women prefer strong men.

Get strong. How? Simple.

There was a course on bodybuilding that was popular in the early 20th century. It was put out by a man who called himself Charles Atlas. The way he sold his course became the stuff of advertising legend.

In the back of comic books would be a one-page comic-style ad, nine panels telling the story of Mac, a creamy and smooth kid at the beach with a girl. A big, burly bully kicks sand in the kid's face. When he can't fight back, the girl is ashamed.

Mac goes back to his place and kicks a chair. He's sick and tired of this! He sends for the Charles Atlas course.

In no time at all, he's buffed up.

He goes back to the beach, sees the bully with his girl, walks up and socks him in the face.

The girl says, "Oh Mac! You ARE a real man after all!"

See?

You can still be purchase the Charles Atlas course. And it is still sound. With a foundation of pushups and crunches and other isometrics, any man can become stronger and improve his physique.

Even men who have a naturally wiry frame can develop strong, ropey muscles. (For a movie example, watch the Westerns Jimmy Stewart made in the 1950s. Stewart successfully transitioned from his early "Aw shucks" image into a tough-as-nails Western hero.)

A real man respects American soldiers

In *Holiday Affair* (1949, dir. Don Hartman), Mitchum works in toys at the department store during the Christmas season. A woman, Janet Leigh, comes in to buy a train set "for my little boy." She is actually a comparison shopper, hired by another store to go around to competitors and check their prices on items.

When she comes back the next day to return the train, Mitchum lets her know he spotted her from the start. He's going to pick up the phone and alert the store detective so her picture will be posted everywhere and she won't be able to do her job. In effect, she'll have to be let go by her employer, and right before Christmas.

She pleads that she really does have a little boy and is his sole support. Mitchum isn't buying the sob story until she gives him enough details to convince him. And when he asks about her husband, she reveals he died in the war.

Mitchum believes her and decides to cut her a break. He won't inform on her but tells her not to come back to his department.

Why does he do it? Because he has respect for war widows and the soldiers who die in battle.

That little act of charity, though, costs Mitchum his job. The floor walker overheard what was going on and Mitchum is given the boot.

Still, he did the right thing. Sometimes that does cost a job, but it's also what keeps your self respect.

There's no price on that.

A man who mocks God does not come to a good end

The Rev. Jonathan Rudd (Robert Mitchum) shows up in small Western town and opens up a church. It just so happens that this event follows the lynching of a card cheat after a game of five card stud, which coincidentally is the title of the film. *5 Card Stud* came out in1968, directed by Henry Hathaway.

Dean Martin plays Van Morgan, a gambler who was part of that ill-fated game. When he tried to stop the lynching he was knocked out cold by Nick Evers (Roddy McDowell).

The other members of the game start to die, one by one, murdered by strangulation.

Somebody is avenging the death of the cheat!

Spoiler alert: If you want to watch the movie and be surprised, don't read on. The film is basically an Agatha Christie-style mystery set in the old West.

And then there were two: Evers and Morgan.

And the killer? Why it's the Rev. Rudd, because the cheat who was lynched was his brother. Rudd has come for revenge, and he's being fed the information on who was involved by the ringleader, Evers! Evers says he is the one who tried to stop the lynching, and Morgan was the real necktie party emcee.

Ah, but at the graveyard where Rudd is laying flowers on his brother's grave, Evers steps out with a gun. He has used Rudd to kill all the players, but held onto the last name, Morgan, until now. He laughs at Rudd, who has figured out that Evers will kill him, kill Morgan, and then be scot-free.

Rudd makes one request, that he be allowed to say a prayer over his brother's grave. Evers lets him. The Rev. Rudd opens his Bible to read a passage of Scripture. The Bible has been hollowed out to hide a gun, which Rudd uses to kill Evers.

At the end, facing Morgan—who has solved the mystery, and knows that Rudd is the killer—Rudd asks if he may read a passage of Scripture.

But Morgan notices the Bible is upside down.

When Rudd tries to shoot, Morgan is ready, and kills Rudd.

A real man does not blaspheme, denigrate, or otherwise mock God. Atheist he may be, but then he's betting against God, and if he turns out to be wrong, he's lost in more ways than one.

A real man respects those who hold to a religious view that is peaceful and loving and charitable. He does not respect someone who does evil in the name of his religion. Nothing is owed there but justice.

My dad, a World War II vet, was not an overtly religious man. My mom, a college graduate and community leader, did not attend church. But they sent me to Sunday School as a kid so I would get the right values seeded in me—love your neighbor, give to those in need, respect authority.

And never dis God.

Once, when I was home from college for Thanksgiving––and into being the typical college twerp who thought he was smarter than his parents––I was asked to say a blessing before the meal, and I half-smiled and addressed God as "The Big Kahuna in the Sky."

When I'd finished my silly prayer, my dad was giving me the same glare I'd known as a kid when I really messed up and disappointed him. He didn't have to say a word. I felt like a complete ass, and deserved to feel that way.

A man who mocks God, though he may not believe, is insecure and immature.

A man apologizes when it's his fault

Real men apologize when they are in the wrong. They don't sentimentalize it, they don't try to manipulate the other side. They say they are sorry, and move on.

And every now and then they show true contrition by cutting off their little finger.

Let me explain.

In *The Yakuza* (1974, dir. Sydney Pollack), Mitchum plays a retired detective who tries to help an old friend. This friend, Tanner (Brian Keith) has been dealing with the yakuza (Japanese mafia), who have kidnapped his daughter. He asks Mitchum, who had post WWII deployment in Japan, to use his contacts there to get Tanner's daughter back.

There's all sorts of backstory intrigue, including a Japanese woman, Eiko (Keiko Kishi) who had loved Mitchum in the old days. She has a brother, Ken (Ken Takakura, an actor sometimes referred to as "the Japanese Robert Mitchum") who is former yakuza. Mitchum asks him for help in getting Tanner's daughter back, even though Ken has kept up a hatred for Mitchum. Just after the war, Ken had been thought dead and Mitchum was the lover of his sister, Eiko. But Ken was not dead and was outraged at this (mainly because of a plot twist. Ken is not Eiko's brother, but her husband!)

Ah, but during the time Ken was thought dead, Mitchum saved Eiko's life. Thus, Ken owes Mitchum a lifelong debt, called *giri*.

Now Mitchum wants to cash that in by getting Ken's help to rescue Tanner's daughter.

Ken has kept in great shape, by the way. He is a *katana* (sword) master. He is no longer yakuza, but in rescuing the girl he kills one of the men of the big yakuza dude, Tono. So now Ken is back in trouble.

All sorts of troubles and death follow, and Ken has to kill his own nephew in self-defense. Bearing this news to his brother, Ken offers to commit *Seppuku*. His brother tells him not to do so. Ken then demonstrates his contrition by way of *yubitsume*, the act of cutting off a portion of the little finger, wrapping it in a cloth, and passing it to the offended party.

Well, all this carnage has come upon Mitchum's former love, Eiko, and her husband, Ken, because of Mitchum himself and his false friend, Tanner (another plot twist there).

So at the very end, having collected on his *giri* from Ken, but causing him so much trouble,

Mitchum performs *yubitsume* and gives his finger to Ken.

Talk about an apology with some meat to it!

The lessons are clear.

First, try not to have anything to do with the *yakuza*. Especially if you're an American.

Second, if something is your fault, apologize and mean it.

A man knows how to be a good loser

A real man knows how to lose.

He doesn't whine about it. He doesn't cry about it. He doesn't curse the winner.

A real man shouldn't be happy about losing, or even complacent.

But once the contest is over, he gets ready for the next one.

He doesn't hang his head and show everybody he's been beaten.

Because a real man knows there is always another game, another challenge, another task.

There used to be honor and dignity in being a good loser.

What that means is you play a game fair and square, you do your best, and if you don't win you congratulate the winner and move on.

In *Rachel and the Stranger* (1948, dir. Norman

Foster), Mitchum plays Jim Fairways, a charming "wilderness man" during colonial America, complete with buckskins, rifle and guitar. He's a friend of David Harvey (William Holden). Harvey, a widower, has just purchased a wife named Rachel (Loretta Young). She's really a "bond servant" (to take care of her father's debt), and that's how Holden treats her, even though she's Loretta Young and has those great eyes. Holden just wants her to do the woman's work and help be a maternal influence on his young son, Davey (Gary Gray).

So here is Holden treating Loretta Young like a servant, out in his wilderness cabin, when Mitchum comes singing along after being off hunting.

He treats Loretta like a lady. He is charming and polite to her, unlike Holden.

It isn't long before he falls for Loretta himself.

He knows that Holden bought her, so he offers Holden money to buy her himself.

To which Loretta becomes rightly outraged.

This is one strong woman. She's had enough of being treated this way. Off she tromps into the forest, and the two men go after her so she doesn't get eaten by a bear or scalped by a hostile.

Around a campfire, Mitchum confesses his love for her and asks her to marry him.

Stuff happens, though, including a battle with Indians who burn down Holden's cabin.

But when everything settles down, Holden confesses his own love for Rachel, who is glad to finally reciprocate.

Which leaves Mitchum out in the cold.

So what does he do?

He loses gracefully. He takes his guitar and rides off singing.

Where is he going? To get himself a wife.

There's always another contest.

A man who preys on the weak is not a real man, and deserves to be taken down

Mitchum's greatest portrayal of a villain is in director Charles Laughton's 1955 classic, *The Night of the Hunter.*

Mitchum plays Harry Powell, a "wolf in sheep's clothing" in the biblical sense—a charlatan preacher who prowls around the Depression-era South preying on widows and depriving them of their money and then their lives. Tattooed on his hands are the words LOVE and HATE, which he uses to illustrate the cosmic battle between innocence and evil.

Despite his consuming hatred, especially toward women and their sexuality, Powell claims to have privileged access to God, practicing a "religion that the Almighty and me worked out betwixt us."

During a stretch in the slammer for car theft, he meets a man (Peter Graves) who recently knocked over a bank and entrusted the $10,000 in stolen loot to his two small children, John and Pearl.

The man eventually receives the death sentence, and Powell, freshly sprung, sets to work insinuating himself into the dead man's community. He woos a gullible, bereaved widow (Shelley Winters) and shortly after marrying her, slits her throat and disposes of the body. Now the children's legal guardian, he interrogates them mercilessly as to the whereabouts of the missing stash. Playing one child against the other, Powell eventually coaxes a confession out of Pearl, who reveals that she's been hiding the money in her doll.

Just as things look hopelessly bleak, the children manage a narrow escape. They flee down the river in a skiff and are eventually discovered by Rachel Cooper (Lillian Gish), a crusty but benign old woman who becomes the children's guardian angel.

She introduces them to the other orphans in her care, feeds them, washes them, and reads to them from the Bible. But the relentless Powell soon tracks them down, and in a scene that gives the film its title, lays siege to the house while Rachel keeps vigil with a shotgun. In an eerie scene charged with symbolic significance, Powell and Rachel sing the hymn "Leaning on the Everlasting Arms" in duet. Powell soon finds his way inside the house, but Gish wings him and calls the police, who take him into custody.

Powell is put on trial and sentenced to death for his crimes, narrowly escaping a local lynch mob, while Rachel and the children hurry home to prepare for Christmas. The film ends with Rachel soliloquizing about the resilience of children ("they abide and they endure") on a snowy, postcard-perfect holiday morning.

To stalk and harm those who are weaker than you is not a mark of manhood. Should a weakling stalk *you*, it may be that you'll need to teach a lesson. But the better course when weaklings snap at your heels is that which is followed by Rick Blaine (Humphrey Bogart) in *Casablanca*. A sniveling little weasel named Ugarte (Peter Lorre) keeps seeking Rick's approval and protection. At one point Ugarte says, "You despise me, don't you, Rick?"

Rick says, "If I gave you any thought I probably would."

Weaklings who yip at true manhood do not deserve your thoughts.

A FINAL WORD ON MANLINESS

What used to be called "manly virtues" have been dismissed and denigrated over the last forty years or more. This acid drip began (as acid drips usually do) in the halls of academia. Gradually the poison seeped into society at large until denigration morphed into accepted wisdom.

But it is the wisdom of fools.

For robust manliness is not only necessary for the vitality of America (*America* as an ideal has also been acid-dripped by the academy), but also for order, civility, protection, and romantic love (if you wonder about this, just take an informal look at what young women on social media are saying about the dearth of real men).

We need a return to the ideal, which was eloquently expressed by President Theodore

Roosevelt in his essay, "The American Boy." Here is an excerpt. I suggest that you read it, frequently, to your sons:

> What we have a right to expect of the American boy is that he shall turn out to be a good American man. Now, the chances are strong that he won't be much of a man unless he is a good deal of a boy. He must not be a coward or a weakling, a bully, a shirk, or a prig. He must work hard and play hard. He must be clean-minded and clean-lived, and able to hold his own under all circumstances and against all comers. It is only on these conditions that he will grow into the kind of American man of whom America can be really proud. ...
>
> No boy can afford to neglect his work, and with a boy work, as a rule, means study. ... I am no advocate of senseless and excessive cramming in studies, but a boy should work, and should work hard, at his lessons—in the first place, for the sake of what he will learn, and in the next place, for the sake of the effect upon his own character of resolutely settling down to learn it. Shiftlessness, slackness, indifference in studying, are almost certain

to mean inability to get on in other walks of life. ...

A boy needs both physical and moral courage. Neither can take the place of the other. ... There is no need to be a prig. There is no need for a boy to preach about his own good conduct and virtue. If he does he will make himself offensive and ridiculous. But there is urgent need that he should practice decency; that he should be clean and straight, honest and truthful, gentle and tender, as well as brave. If he can once get to a proper understanding of things, he will have a far more hearty contempt for the boy who has begun a course of feeble dissipation, or who is untruthful, or mean, or dishonest, or cruel, than this boy and his fellows can possibly, in return, feel for him. The very fact that the boy should be manly and able to hold his own, that he should be ashamed to submit to bullying without instant retaliation, should, in return, make him abhor any form of bullying, cruelty, or brutality. ...

Bullies do not make brave men; and boys or men of foul life cannot become good citizens, good Americans, until they change; and even after the change scars will be left on their souls.

The boy can best become a good man by being a good boy—not a goody-goody boy, but just a plain good boy. I do not mean that he must love only the negative virtues; I mean he must love the positive virtues also. "Good," in the largest sense, should include whatever is fine, straightforward, clean, brave, and manly. ... A healthy-minded boy should feel hearty contempt for the coward, and even more hearty indignation for the boy who bullies girls or small boys, or tortures animals. One prime reason for abhorring cowards is because every good boy should have it in him to thrash the objectionable boy as the need arises.

Of course the effect that a thoroughly manly, thoroughly straight and upright boy can have upon the companions of his own age, and upon those who are younger, is incalculable. If he is not thoroughly manly, then they will not respect him, and his good qualities will count for but little; while, of course, if he is mean, cruel, or wicked, then his physical strength and force of mind merely make him so much the more objectionable a member of society. He cannot do good work if he is not strong and does not try with his whole heart and soul to count in any contest; and his strength will be a curse to himself and to every one else if he does not have thorough command over himself and over his own evil passions, and if he does not use his strength on the side of decency, justice, and fair dealing.

In short, in life, as in a foot-ball game, the principle to follow is:

Hit the line hard; don't foul and don't shirk, but hit the line hard!

TOP TEN ROBERT MITCHUM PERFORMANCES

For those of you who don't know much about the work of Robert Mitchum, you have a treat in store. To start you off, here are my top ten favorite Mitchum performances, in ascending order:

10. The Story of G. I. Joe

The movie that made Mitchum an actor of note in Hollywood. His last soliloquy near the end is a master class in how to deliver an emotional speech without chewing scenery. Somewhere along the way Mitchum learned the most valuable lesson about movie acting there is: say your lines and don't bump into anything. You will never catch Mitchum overacting.

9. Farewell, My Lovely

An older, world-weary Mitchum makes a perfect Philip Marlowe, the L.A. PI created by Raymond Chandler. He has the noir look (always did) and the perfect voice for the narration. Winston Churchill, who became Prime Minister of England at age 65, at just the right time to lead his country against the Nazis, said his whole life had seemed a preparation for that moment. It seems that all of Mitchum's acting life had prepared him for playing Marlowe.

8. Thunder Road

This was a personal project for Mitchum, who came up with the original story, stars (with his son), co-produced, and co-wrote the awesome theme song. A year later, Mitchum recorded the ballad he wrote for the film.

7. The Friends of Eddie Coyle

Mitchum plays an aging, low-level criminal who is facing a prison stretch. He doesn't want to go, as he has a wife and children he is responsible for. The plot takes place in Boston, and Mitchum even puts on a Boston accent with just the right touch, better even than the over-zealous Beantown tones of Ben Affleck in *The Town.*

6. The Night of the Hunter

Mitchum's portrayal of the blustering villain Harry Powell is masterful, moving from cartoonish preacher to vile killer in the blink of an eye. He deliciously delivers such lines as, "No, no, don't you touch that, little lamb! Don't touch my knife. That makes me mad. That makes me very, very mad!" And: "Open that door, you spawn of the devil's own strumpet!"

5. Ryan's Daughter

This sprawling David Lean film, beautifully filmed in Ireland, was considered a flop when it first appeared. But time has been kinder to it, and Mitchum's against-type portrayal of a sensitive school teacher is the best thing in the film.

4. Cape Fear

The menace that is Max Cady (Mitchum) is perhaps the greatest portrait of a psychopath ever put on film. Not because it is over-the-top, but because it seems so *real.*

3. Heaven Knows, Mr. Allison

Mitchum really gets to show off his acting chops in this one, along with another great star of the era, Deborah Kerr.

2. Home from the Hill

Underrated as a film, Mitchum's performance as the troubled patriarch of a southern family is supremely moving. Mitchum manages to be vulnerable without being soft. Quite an achievement.

1. Out of the Past

Quite simply, this is one of the best (many critics say *the* best) of the entire film noir genre. Mitchum inhabits this role as naturally as he fills out a trench coat. If you had to choose one performance to preserve for the future so people catch the very essence of Robert Mitchum, this would be it.

AUTHOR'S NOTE

Thank you for reading *Manliness: The Robert Mitchum Way.*

For a book like this to have the reach that it should, it needs reviews from happy readers. If this describes you, then I would consider it an enormous favor if you would leave a review of the book so it may find a wider audience. Simple click the link below (you may be asked to sign in to your Amazon account). Thanks so much!

Click here to leave a review for Manliness: The Robert Mitchum Way

ABOUT THE AUTHOR

JAMES SCOTT BELL is a winner of the International Thriller Writers Award and the #1 bestselling author of books on the craft of fiction. He studied writing with Raymond Carver at the University of California, Santa Barbara, and graduated with honors from the University of Southern California Law Center.

A former trial lawyer, Jim writes full time in his home town of Los Angeles.

For More Information
JamesScottBell.com

THRILLERS BY JAMES SCOTT BELL

The Mike Romeo Thriller Series

Romeo Series Page

"Mike Romeo is a terrific hero. He's smart, tough as nails, and fun to hang out with. James Scott Bell is at the top of his game here. There'll be no sleeping till after the story is over." - **John Gilstrap**, New York Times bestselling author of the Jonathan Grave thriller series

The Ty Buchanan Legal Thriller Series

#1 Try Dying
#2 Try Darkness
#3 Try Fear

"Part Michael Connelly and part Raymond Chandler, Bell has an excellent ear for dialogue and makes contemporary L.A. come alive. Deftly plotted, flawlessly executed, and compulsively readable, Bell takes his place among the top authors in the field. Highly recommended." - **Sheldon Siegel**, *New York Times* bestselling author

Stand Alone Thrillers

Long Lost

No More Lies

Blind Justice

Don't Leave Me

Your Son is Alive

Final Witness

Framed

www.ingramcontent.com/pod-product-compliance
Lightning Source LLC
Chambersburg PA
CBHW022340280326
41934CB00006B/719